NAKED
   LADIES
       ON THE
              ROAD

NAKED LADIES ON THE ROAD

poems by

Mike Sutin

SUNSTONE PRESS

SANTA FE

© 2005 by Mike Sutin. All rights reserved.

All rights to poems previously published in magazines, chapbooks, and books are either retained by the publisher or author as previously reserved, and all poems that are being published for the first time in this volume have all reprint rights to the author. These rights include any means of recording or reproducing the material through oral or visual means, including videotape, photocopying, film, and records.

No part of this book may be reproduced in any form or by any electronic or mechanical means including information storage and retrieval systems without permission in writing from the publisher, except by a reviewer who may quote brief passages in a review.

Sunstone books may be purchased for educational, business, or sales promotional use. For information please write: Special Markets Department, Sunstone Press, P.O. Box 2321, Santa Fe, New Mexico 87504-2321.

Library of Congress Cataloging-in-Publication Data:

Sutin, Mike.
  Naked ladies on the road : poems / by Mike Sutin.
    p. cm.
  ISBN 0-86534-435-3 (pbk. : alk. paper)
  1. Santa Fe (N.M.)—Poetry. I. Title.

PS3619.U884N35 2005
811'.6—dc22

                                              2005016081

WWW.SUNSTONEPRESS.COM
SUNSTONE PRESS / POST OFFICE BOX 2321 / SANTA FE, NM 87504-2321 /USA
(505) 988-4418 / *ORDERS ONLY* (800) 243-5644 / FAX (505) 988-1025

To Agnew, Ev & Joe, Jr.

CONTENTS

PREFACE / 11

ACKNOWLEDGEMENTS AND THANKS / 17

CANYON ROAD CHRONICLES / 21

Naked Ladies on the Road / 23
Planted in a Good Acre / 27
You've Just Got to Love Their Lingo / 28
    (The Way We Are/Were)
Artwalk / 30
Canyon Road / 31
The Saga of Gypsy Alley / 32
The Canyon Road Gallery Scene (Shit Happens) / 35
High Walls / 36
Luminarias / 37
Avocado / 38
DeVargas and the Canyon Road (The Fiesta Run) / 40

ONE BLOCK NORTH AND ONE BLOCK SOUTH / 41

Santa Fe River / 43
How Santa Klaus Came to the Kremlin / 44
Plumbing Crisis / 46
Epitaph for Escondido / 47
La Acequia Madre (The Mother Ditch) / 48
Rites of Passage / 49
City Different Drought / 50

PAST ATALAYA THE PATHS TO PECOS LEAD BUT TO THE BRAVES / 51

El Camino del Cañon / 53
Out to the Randall Davey / 54
The Ridges of Santa Fe County / 55
On First Looking into Chapman's Boner / 56
Chapman's Road (Paso por Aquí) / 57
Remarks at Pecos National Monument / 58

OUTPOSTS / 59

Melting in the Dark, 1-5 / 61
Living in the Lap of Luxury. It's for the Birds / 66

THE GOOD, THE BAD, AND THE UGLY / 73

NOTES ON THE POEMS / 81

PREFACE

The neighborhood through which Santa Fe's Canyon Road runs suffers from city schizophrenia.

Residences, whether modest or palatial, all enjoy market values far over reasonable New Mexico values. As our real estate brokers tell us: location is everything. Owners fantasize of the possibility of sliding into commercial uses, which translate into higher value and rents, while at the same time maintaining quiet, peaceful, neighborly, residential living space.

Canyon Road, once the domain of resident artists, families, mud huts, and small shopkeepers, has become a creeping commercial dreadnought of high-density, high-traffic, high-end sophisticated art galleries and restaurants, with land values and rent high beyond imagination. Potential commercial users covet residential areas.

Midway between the Acequia Madre (mother irrigation ditch) and the Santa Fe River and within easy walking distance of the historic downtown plaza, Canyon Road attracts both visitors and locals. In a state where poverty levels are also high, the average downtown hotel room rates are reported to be higher than those in seven major tourist cities.

The poems you will read took shape within this framework.

In the eyes of some, Santa Fe has become a national treasure, a high-desert Disneyland, a small city in search of an identity, "tourist town U.S.A.," a caricature of itself. Santa Fe is marketed as a multi-cultural, artistic, high-tech infomesa, a high-thought, book-buying, laid-back, dress-down, animal- and-peace-loving, liberal, live-and-let-live, playground paradise in which the world is wonderful, the weather is wonderful, the light is legend, small businesses are locally gardened, and as the place to get and be high. All these images are projected to the outside.

Often overlooked to the dismay of the over-confident and the oblivious (those who live without Santa Fe's invisible world) is the community's deep and fervent religious and racial roots that are passionately preserved and protected. See the title poem. They don't call it the City of the Holy Faith for nothing.

The City's strength lies in a cornucopia of cacophonous and quirky characters contending, complaining, cajoling like an uncontrolled chorus in a small town hall meeting, and communicating through all available channels, many with a reverence for preservation in all its societal and cultural aspects. They are free-spirited, expressive, devotional people and activists on both sides of many issues. Let's open up an argument in Santa Fe. Choices exist for the voices of the people, people who are doing all those things that are normally expected of human beings. The poems capture and capsulize some wonders and some warts.

This, my second published volume of poetry, continues to reflect a preference for, but not strict adherence to, formal and traditional English versification that uses metrical patterns and the device of rhyme to heighten effectiveness and, in the absence of either, at least some rhythmic quality. The use of lines that are pleasing to the ear do not create limitations on expression.

Understanding poetry is often difficult. The ear of the 21st century is not tuned. The meaning of many poems is not easily accessible. Some of the poems in this volume offer references to assist the reader. These references are found near the end of this volume. A poem need not have meaning. The meaning need not be evident. As discussed in the *Broadview Anthology of Poetry*, one school of thought suggests that "meaning should inhere in the poem's expressive and sensuous qualities, not in some explicit statement or versified idea" and that "expressiveness works through figurative rather than literal modes." Others look to poetry for insights into the "nature of human experience, and expect elevated thought in carefully wrought language." Some of the concepts expressed in my poems may offend, because of what may seem to be moralistic or didactic or judgmental expression. Suggestion has been made that an appropriate subtitle should be "feces, species and coprophilia." Many have stepped in it.

A prominent poet, William Everson, has written:

> *As a genre political poetry is both didactic and rhetorical. To be effective it must be intensely involved and ideologically committed, though such commitment must be moderated by intellectual discrimination, moral courage, and, sometimes, irony. Within these bounds it is best when it is extreme: intemperate, explosive, and scornful. Indeed, unless it invokes the leap for the jugular, we are not apt to pay much attention to it. Only when it shocks with relevance can it change the course of human inertia. Being poetry, it must be concentrated and blistering rather than rational and discursive, or we will cling to prose and remain in dispassionate*

analysis. As an axiom it can be said that the rougher political poetry is, the better we will like it, or, if it opposes our own predilections, the more deeply will we fear it. Political poetry speaks to the mind, certainly, but at least it speaks through the mind to the passion. In spite of ourselves, hearing it, we are moved.

    I was first a sports writer and I am now a lawyer, having practiced some 46 years with a heavy concentration in business and economic development and having published a number of legal articles in national and local venues. I have run long races and climbed high mountains. It is hard to know how poetry grabbed me to provide a release from the strain of daily life in all its professional, health, and familial components.

    I love to think about things around me and to express in poems how I feel about them, feelings that seem to be universally enjoyed. I feel blessed that my daily life is haunted by poetic images. Yes, it is therapeutic, but it is also something more. I hope the poems evoke and provoke your emotions, for that is the purpose of poetry.

    I thank my wife Esther for hanging in there with me, reading and correcting the manuscript, and designing the cover and all interior artwork. I thank Rose, whose fingers have lingered over these poems for years, and Ahza for fine-tuning. I thank Jim Smith for publishing this book, more than he will ever know.

    And, thanks for reading.

Mike Sutin
Santa Fe, New Mexico
August 2005

ACKNOWLEDGMENTS AND THANKS

For permission to use the cover page photographs, acknowledgment and thanks are made to the following:

For "Children's Fountain" originally installed in DeVargas Park, Santa Fe, New Mexico, to the sculptor, Linda Strong.

For "Innermost," to the sculptor, Malcolm Alexander.

For permission to publish or reproduce the poems in this volume, acknowledgment and thanks are made to the following:

For "Naked Ladies on the Road," to the author, Guadalupe Villegas (pseudonym), and Gershon Siegel and Linda Braun, publishers, from *Eldorado Sun*, Vol. 216.

For "The Canyon Road Gallery Scene," to the author, Calderon Chichicastanega (pseudonym), and *New Frontiers of New Mexico*, the publisher, from *New Frontiers of New Mexico*. © by New Frontiers of New Mexico.

For "High Walls," to the author, Moises C. de Baca (pseudonym), and New Frontiers of New Mexico, the publisher, from *New Frontiers of New Mexico*. © by New Frontiers of New Mexico.

For "DeVargas and the Canyon Road" and "Out to the Randall Davey," to the author and to the Santa Fe Striders, the publisher of *Mile Markers*.

For "Avocado," to the author, Joaquin de la Raza (pseudonym), and publisher, *The Sun*.

CANYON ROAD CHRONICLES

Naked Ladies on the Road[1]

The flagrant naked ladies of this Road
offend no known moral Canyon creed,
produce no prudish riot episode,
and satisfy some high aesthetic need.

For freedom, seek out neither church nor state;
instead, hang it all out in private parts
where it will either fail or sail (with freight).
O Muse! The market place protects the arts.

The artist's song is often sadly sung,
a gorilla nailed up on the arcane cross,
the holy mother's breast in dung,
the sublimated wish of Thanatos.

"Our Lady" in rose petalled bikini
held aloft by a bare breasted saint
is portrayed as a polynesian wahine,
hardly an image of artistic restraint.

To what purpose this computer collage
if not be to enhance Her décolletage?
A vision of Virgin so scantily clad
is modeled on t-shirts, low riders, mouse pads.

Bare breasted bouncing boobs a-jiggling
with jew-star pasties suggest Ringling,
not hate; what weight the internal intent,
for who-in-the-hell cares what really was meant?

We see what we see and we feel what we feel
when we see La Lupita beginning to peel.
To battle, we offer familial baggage
and cannot discern God's beauty from garbage.

The racial card is played to circumvent
outsiders in the City Different
by Hispano defenders of the faith
who protesteth because their Lord thus saith.

Can we by our numbers cause freedom to fail,
keep pubic from public and lock both in jail?
So let's cut their balls off, then their grant money;
they'll crawl back on their knees, tongues hungry for
   honey.

Perhaps the image of the woman strong
of limb reminds too much of first Eve's song,
and mini-skirts and combat boots creates a fear in him
of temptress, puta, nympho and virginia slim.

Portrayed and dressed in dissimilar styles
on hoods by hoods and fingernail files,
on glow-in-the dark, four on the floor, gear shift glass
   knobs
and other people-pragmatic thingumabobs,

This Chicana woman is just a part of me,
another female body yearning to be free.
My goddess of fertility is a crescent moon
to which the Aztecs sacrificed au clair de lune.

But how benign the much maligned bikini!
In history, retold by the maven J. Orsini,
no burning bush, the graven image idol cult,
becomes an icon, masses now exult.

When I am old, I shall wear a floral bathing suit,
and run for mayor or a pubic orifice,
but my bishop will call me a bad prostitute
and call for Catholic protests and the Hispanos to hiss.

He's offended by our lapse of moral turpitude
in the face of my phantom female pulchritude.
I'm sick of race hate talk from Ortiz-like-type dudes
who have no respect for The Beatitudes.

"Tear it down," "take it off," my people insist.
Let's now excise it, this festering cyst.
Our faith is quite strong, but why does the State
encourage religious insult and hate?

It is the height of all hypocrisies
to minimize my blessed mother in her B.V.D.s,
with money massed from taxes for museums,
like Christians chewed by lion cats in coliseums.

La Virgen is the female god to whom I daily pray,
to let me be a woman in a woman sort of way.
A capital G she is to me, religiously,
and so I flaunt my femininity, obnoxiously.

And did the holy mother use her tongue;
and was the guadalupe virgin brown;
and how well was the pale prophet hung;
upon whom did the lamb of g-d go down?

Or was our holy mother's skin bone black?
The mind-near-madness twitches tightly strung
between greenback and ego's lack of tact.
Has evil from the pen and paint brush sprung?

Not thorns, but wire barbs star stud his crown,
the jesus jew far, far from middletown;
and, on the Road, the wit of spirit sprints unwrung,
among the galleries, old and young.

Can those who choose to worship womankind
and man as Gods protest the painter's mind
that centers on big boobs and on what's behind;
for, in the urbane viewer's eye, all buff is blind.

True spirit takes no fashion figure form
and eludes allegiance to a common norm.
The human bod allures with scents and curves
and titillates our reproductive nerves.

From ink and white sable fiber brush and bristles
bursts tigers of the sabre-tooth and thistles.
The music of the mind of man can find no rest
from fanatical fingers of the self-possessed.

And yet, so long as art creators proscribe bounds,
their thrust-out chins will be exposed to faith's
   hellhounds.

Planted in a Good Acre

blond, nordic, youthful types
still, frozen mannequins
blinded catatonic zombies
cast hard within this grassy yard
stop-gapped in the public urban garden glen
and not long in time from the black forest fen

grotesque, greenish ghost-tykes
and other ghastly look alikes
pulled along in four-wheeled wagons
at playground with the dark Reich's
doberman foam-mouthed dragons
now wrought-iron gate leashed against the world

…but waiting

You've Just Got to Love Their Lingo[2]
(The Way We Are/Were)

Señor Antonio totters,
tentatively, wobbly,
amidst a pack of refugees
in their tight fit après-skis,
toward a wizened Vigil
upon an ancient Mayans' log,
searching for a sun-warmed
south winter wall against
which to rest his hoary back,
eighty años bent of age
and other decaying processes.

In summer, Señor Moya sits,
in sleeveless undershirt,
high upon his cement stoop,
last resident descendant
of the past, and oversees
hoards of tourists trooping
up and down the city's soul
and wonders when neon will, too,
soon supplant his home
into bursting glory-hype
upon the moving art walk stage
and other decaying processes.

You've just got to love their lingo.
I love it when they say their
"holy ave san Marias," and
"the aspens are turning amarillas
en las sangrias." I suppose

we gringos have our Ringos, too,
juxtaposed against their
expansive Pancho Villas
and other ranchos grandes
gallerias laced with las vegas.

On el calle canyones, on Fridays,
Ms. Maggie Geffert proudly jogs
las fiestas (as the town folk
dutifully applaud, shout,
and consume chili curry
ratatouilles
in coyote-type cafés) all the way
up to the Randall Davey,
as if she were a racing star,
and crazy lady Claude raises
and cooks small pet shop dogs
right next to the margaritas bar
in the room where the locos
all hang out
(O! It was quite a scandal, baby),
among other decaying processes.

Artwalk

Who will clean up the clear plastic cups
cracked underfoot and kicked along
the concrete gutters of camino escondido
in the canyon corridor between croft's
and claiborne and the arts and crafts
once residential rabbit warrens that attract
with the aura of instant alley culture?

Who will clean up the crunchy
cauliflower and cucumber cream dip
dripped from plastic-coated
cream-coloured plates by would be
cumberbunded compound collectors of schlock
seeking sociability while rubbing up against
the jeans-clad baseball capped tie-dyed crowd?

In the eighties, we got cabernet and chardonnay,
catered cakes and camembert coated crackers
served up by cocktail waitresses at the upscale places.
Now, we celebrate the success of each weekly repeat
with calistoga soda,
poured out by penny-protecting percentage pirates
sparingly filling their quota.

Canyon Road

Where once a sacred streetscape stood unscathed
in glory days of golden dust, sun-bathed
in its adobe innocence unswathed,
now seethes an outdoor market place for fleas,
infested rugs, ceramic mugs, kinetic sleaze,
paraded one-way with auto-splashing freeze
on moms and strollers bereft of paved sidewalks.
Red ristras, tie-dyed tees the shop girl hawks
where the forlorn ghost of Claude's bistro stalks.

The way that celebrates with civic pride
exports a Persian magic carpet ride.
In draped adobe walls is taste denied.
The city's well-sold faith in art and soul
is not a place to take a holy stroll.
While up and down calm residential streets,
the cloud of crass commercialism creeps
from house to house with wares and hype so tacky
it seems that zoning's once good sense went wacky.

Father culture, to whom the tourists pray:
restore to us our former fine art way
to seek big bucks with which the Texans pay.
While underfoot, find freshly murdered turds
whose deaths are left unmourned by poets' words.
This ancient trail crowned by a black-topped Road
is half a prince and half an ugly toad.
O Truth of Muse, thy tongue is touched with woeful
  warts
when contemplating concepts of the Canyon's arts.

The Saga of Gypsy Alley[3]

The Camino has no trash cans
and no dog walkers scoop the poop
from cracked sidewalks and cluttered curbs
where tourists tramp for art and craft.

Old path pollutes with dumpsters
that overflow with plastic bags
of black that reek of stink and slime.
O brother, can you spare a dime?

Misshapen metal shell-struck landing craft
like Omaha beached monster alley;
no place for strolls or eating out,
a street of crap for all to see.

If your walked doggie drops its doo
upon the pathways in plain view,
the city judge will brown hat you,
to mollify the thankful few,
restrain your arms and legs in stocks
and yellow star a feckless jew,
to purify the people's blocks.

O! Milton la calle hath need of thee
at this unconvincing hour
to save this neighborhood gone sour,
from refuse of the kitchen galley.

Alas and farewell Gypsy Alley,
and good-bye lair of the red wolves,
to ateliers of artistries
and the lure of painter elves.

Death comes in many different ways
to the ancient calle cañon.
When old man Vigil said good-bye
and shipped his soul to greater sky,
his Mayans' log was left unshrined,
but no one else can sit upon
or fill his body space for him,
and who will fill the interim?

Where once we went in winter
when the tourists were away,
is now replaced by plaza rents
instead of oil and lead-based scents.
In place of art, they're making hay.

The manor lord elucidates:
"We saved this space from condo life,"
but left our artists' lives in strife.

"I sell not much of art that's good.
Our scene has been misunderstood;
and beauty's out, not on the edge.
To honor technique's a sacrilege

"of all postmodern hippy hop
that creates chaos without rule
and causes collectors not to shop;
subjects modernity to ridicule.

"We limit sacred white wall space
to deco, folk and in your face
that deal with current social issues
like pubic hairs, Oñate statues.

"We're just about ten years behind
the worst works of the human mind.
But never fear, we will catch up:
papooses in the wickiup.

"That's why I chose to close the door,
to help assuage the public's pain;
but pity not a plight of poor;
I'll swap commission for long-term gain."

The Canyon Road Gallery Scene
(Shit Happens)

Often emanating from artful opening offerings
is the aura of awful opening offalings;
that which can be deeply felt at friday art house
 hoppings
is typified by friendly field mouse droppings.

High Walls

Don't let the mud huts throw you.
The prices are as high inside as
the stuccoed walls that hide from
view the pot roast, the pottery,
and the potted plants; take your
pick of the Picassos, the curried
rices, chili and exotic spices,
sauteed chicken livers, racks of
stylish posters, or the stacks of
fancy photographs spread out on
walnut window sills.

Rains and time melt all walls into
hills. Adobe rivers and rotted ruins
will strut no peacocked plaques
putting on airs in praise of high
livers, part time, put together,
polished, propertied patrons of the arts and
eating, who protect these pretensed mud shacks,
encircled by wagons of tall walls,
riding shotgun at high noon in the
swirling swill of the spittoon,
surrounded by packs of snapping coyotes
and sharp-toothed snakes.

Luminarias

At Navidad, before the yankee
Kearney disgraced our sacred race
and put our culture in its place,
catolicos all lit the way
so shepherds seeking Jesus birth
could find the path to holy earth.

Uncomplicated by dissents
for relics, masses, popes or saints,
everybody did this thing
and it was all the same to us,
for church and state and home were one
when darkness came with setting sun.

With dry woodpiles prepared as pyres
and candles upon church and spires,
the glow and splendor of the light
made this event a righteous night,
unlike these little bags of sand,
symbolic of a faithless land.

Avocado

They call me tio taco.
Among my people;
this expresses disenchantment
with my just not saying "no"
to division and development.

(Green grow the lilacs, O)

Years ago,
I made fast tracks
out of the barrio de analco,
snaring lucrative commissions
on fast fax sales
of the ancestral casitas
of my former vecinos
to whom the lure of quick silver
was too great an urge to overcome,

(Green grow the lilacs, O)

and the fragile
beings of whose old
care-ridden mamacitas,
shriveled like an over-ripe avocado,
could be better served
within a residencia
group setting.

(Green grow the lilacs, O)

At least, that is what
they were clearly betting
when they sold,
and fled the colonia,
in favor of the eastside;
and, it is said,
they never admitted any transgression,
at confession,
en iglesia,
en catechize,
or otherwise.

(Green grow the lilacs, O)

Not unlike an oreo,
I may also be brown on the outside,
but a little green-go on the inside,

(Green grow the lilacs, O)

and I always vote for progress,
as a rule,
and my children stand tall
in preparatory school
and drive range rovers
when they cruise Cerrillos
(if they ever cruise at all).

(Green grow the lilacs, O)

DeVargas and the Canyon Road
(The Fiesta Run)

I did not run your race this year.
Where I should be seemed fairly clear.
My legs won't churn at racing pace
and produce results like: last in place.
Instead, I turned to mountain trail
to earn release from urban jail.
To celebrate conquest of clans
is not a spot for also-rans,
but needs a festive taste to win,
all honor to the victor's kin.
The force of youth enjoys such play,
while aging seeks another day.
The solitude of silent hills
supplants the pavement's asphalt frills,
and slow move up on one's own legs
is laurel's phase on life's late stage.

ONE BLOCK NORTH AND ONE BLOCK SOUTH

Santa Fe River

The season's rest erodes no rounded river rocks.
Wild wind rips canyon passages
and swirls all black dead debris in its depths;
raw whips dry dirt on plastic bags
where empty cans of diet coke submerge
as garbaged silt in weakened state.
No rio waters flow in winter term.
The snow wet melt is stopped by freeze,
as peaks produce the ice-packed earthen checks
while decay darkens buried poet's ink.
Cold heaps of soggy decomposing leaves
of hibernating trees clog run-off drains
which dream at night of roots and rubbers when
the Santa Fe River is starting to run.

How Santa Klaus Came to the Kremlin[5]

This story's of an overpass:
My moniker is Dave Greenglass.
I fried my sis for my wife's ass.
But now I use another name
to write a book to shift the blame
where it belonged—on me,
to right a wrong in history.
I'm out of jail to pen a plot,
but want my name to be forgot.

The secrets schemed from Fuchs to Gold
and by this means our souls were sold,
all players in the War called Cold.
One long block north from Canyon Road
were passed the plans to bomb implode,
across a stream called Santa Fe
(as Russian spies, we lost our way),
a bridge across well-treasoned waters,
red-hot seat for Israel's daughters.

The U.S. liked to burn Hebrews,
but that's not hardly timely news;
the whole world wants to kill the Jews.
This river called the Holy Faith
(when it runs, world wonder eighth)
is now spanned by the bridge Delgado,
a long, long way from Red Moscow.
My motives are as clear as glass.
My book sells well, grows green like grass.

Before I age and have to go,
I need to square a fiasco.
This truth does not depend on dough.
The cloak-and-dagger deed was done
at four, well-sheltered from the sun,
upon the Castillo viaduct;
and there America was fucked.
Castillo bridge is falling down
to modernize the City brown.

Unlike a priceless pot site shard,
the cement's in a building yard.
The wooden beams died just as hard,
for now they serve as yard landscaping,
victimized by new town raping.
This ode to overpass is ended.
We players into hell descended:
how Santa Klaus came to the Kremlin?
The U.S.A. was grabbed by a gremlin,
by a lone spy called Perseus,
who could be any one of us.

Plumbing Crisis[4]

There's a pueblo in your plumbing.
The potsherds prospects are quite numbing.
The mountain of the Lord is rumbling.
Jericho, thy walls are crumbling.
The clogged up line stops water coming.
The backed up sludge is slowly scumming.
There's thunder in the ancient plumbing.
Hear the ancients faintly drumming?

Epitaph for Escondido[6]

The sun is starting to sink in the south.
Zozobra ignites from his feet to his mouth.
A hint of chill pervades dawn's early light.
The tourists have taken their vacation home flight.
The season's pink cosmos, purple asters sideshow.
Fragile apache plume frequent the dry arroyo,
and apricots fall and ferment in the earth,
while pungent chamisas give golden-tipped birth.
Rios's piñon pine is piling up high.
The crystalline color of blue composes the sky.
From chimneys of wood stoves, the kindling burns slow,
as aspen leaves take flight and fade to dull yellow,
and bright-orange flowers on ditchside globe mallow.
Our autumn is quiet and contemplative time,
a time for putting up chile, picking carmine apples,
collecting grapes from the vine,
a time to mud plaster adobe, protecting from winter winds' whine
and creating metered pastoral poetry in rhyme.
The wafting aroma of roasting green,
of smoke vapors filtering from the fireplace screen,
an altogether lamentable sub-alpine scene—
for, where old folks slowly stroll and joyful children shout,
there is no joy in Mudvilla,
for tiny Escondido has struck out.

La Acequia Madre[7]
(The Mother Ditch)

Our ancestors sought
certain sanctity symbols
in search of answers, ancient sites,
in search of ancient rites,
a sort of holy way of keeping ditches clean.
And so we celebrate arabia's acequias
from the first at old Chamita
near now abandoned Santa Cruz,
where rivers ran like runner's shoes,
to the center of the City Different
whose water ways gave way to cars and pavement,
presumably for public betterment.

When Colonel Kearney's Codex killed our sacred rights,
when in anger, anguish and despair,
we grow too old to sanely care,
when times become too mean and hard,
we do not hold back, and boldly play the race and culture card
to stir the soul of La Raza's bard.
We mourn in reflected sacramental candle light
for times when prayer, hard work and water were the glues,
and there were no alternatives from which to choose.
By the mother's waters we sat down and wept
for ways, now memories our minds have swept,
and promises unkept.

Rites of Passage[8]

Privacy's an accomplished act.
The frost confirms the fateful fact:
firm fences fortify our friends,
and all good trails must have their ends.

Our babes and western cultures creep
and leave old ways to those who weep.
The certainties of time will savage
once-held beliefs in rights of passage.

And on the dusty militar,
the hills now seem much more afar.
Lord, leave us as we were before.
Where is our cid compeador?

City Different Drought

This city's gone from seed to weed too soon.
We bake beneath the sun and dry our days,
like white men staked upon a pebbled hill
of ants at noon and crowned with honeyed sap
to lure and satiate the visitor
whose mandibles devour sights like soft flesh.
To water deep relieves the grief of earth.

PAST ATALAYA
THE PATHS TO
PECOS LEAD BUT
TO THE BRAVES

El Camino del Cañon[9]

They curbed and guttered Canyon Road,
produced a prince from a horny toad.

Long way to come from the short path to Pecos,
from adobe mudhuts to a tourist oasis

of straw and sand and clay four inches thick,
the art and soul of soil and earthen brick.

This was the firewood route of el burro.
The calle now collects chiaroscuro.

Once watered, our orchards, from fickle la madre,
our old ways run dry from asphalt hot pavé.

They curbed and guttered Canyon Road,
produced a prince from a horny toad.

Out to the Randall Davey

And where have all the dead leaves gone,
on this, my run past Audubon?
Winter's sharp wind whips hard Fall's brown
leaves of dying trees in frenzied terror
to farmers' fields bereft of sheaves,
to curbs and sides of sapless streets.
To save myself from mental error,
I must push on to get to town
before I freeze in drifts up to my knees.
What happens when the oven overheats?
Cold weather shrivels fallen leaves,
full twists the skeletons in breeze
like cast cement contorts death's mask
and mixes ice and snow to mash,
then dries to pulverized gray dust
like six million souls reduced to ash,
in circumstances then considered just,
with ovens by which flesh and bones combust.
Like leaves left to molder in the sun,
the jews have no place left to run.

The Ridges of Santa Fe County

I have this very secret friend
I met not far from Chapman's bend,
about half way up Atalaya.
In passing there, we say "hi ya,"
as I go up and she goes down
the mountain just outside of town.

Her hip is inflamed at the joint
that causes pause at trail's mid point.
I think she dreams of island boys
with whom she dallies before she toys.

We also thought of death that day
(the hill's a complex place to play);
for her, her mom; for me, my legs.
The forest's filled with fears and plagues
of hantavirus, rats and fleas.
I have arthritis of the knees.

A newborn hole infests her soul.
No-fun fixations for a stroll,
an early Sunday morning run.
We wonder just what race we've won.

On First Looking into Chapman's Boner

Felled pines do not whisper;
neither do they thunder
nor roar.
The land that god has planted,
let no man put asunder.
Wind ripples softly lisp
upon the shore
of remembrance;
soft sucking nurture from the nipples
of nature;
not any more;
before man, these were trees.

Chapman's Road
(Paso por Aquí)

No rust turbo tractor caterpillar chrysalis
shall ever transform this corrupted riderless
road into a monarch butterfly.

Neither contractor nor conservation trust
nor other occasional passers-by
shall ever recast this mountain land.

Crunching crushing grinding
crunching crushing grinding
crunching crushing grinding

pieces of pebbles into smaller pebbles
and smaller pebbles into particles of sand,
eroding aeons of rock to earth,

smaller pebbles poking pesty holes
in the soles of plodding shoes of time,
from time to time and throughout time.

Remarks at Pecos National Monument[10]

Some eight score years ago, our fathers left
their homes right here and walked to Walatoa
and left the bones of their beloved dead at rest
within the walls of this once populated place.
We will not speak today of those who thought that science
gave them the right to disturb this hallowed ground
to disinter, to probe, to pick, to crack
apart our forebears' skeletons,
unsepulcher our gourds, potsherds and even turds.
Our sneakered feet are sore and seared and blistered,
small sacrifice for sacred obligation.
At sunrise, we walkers moved more briskly.
From black asphalt sun-baked-heat battle zone,
we reversed track, returned to this, our former Pecos home.
For eighty miles, we marched toward making history.
We are a moral and symbolic victory.
Remains in boxes, grave goods, announce arrival
to celebrate our ancient ancestors' survival
and of our race as people ascended from the earth.
Thank you.

OUTPOSTS

Melting in the Dark 1 [11]

Two statues stood for years in Vargas Park,
turned on to fun when the water's warm
and turned off at winter's nocturnal dark.
But now, it seems, there's cause for great alarm.

The squirt once shot by Bud now propels lead,
and Sis has finally bought the farm.
And those whose minds decline with senses fled
insist on offing the offending arm.

So eye for eye and tooth for tooth is key.
Bud's rights are now reduced to barren arms.
Good sense gives way to sensitivity.
But Sis is clearly free of contrived harms.

Melting in the Dark 2 [12]

…except, of course, for that one-eyed red snake,
uncurled from out between her brother's legs,
that caused a close community to break
from fear of garden Eden's serpent dregs.

How could a hose of forged metallic
be mistaken for a sculpture phallic?
Among the ancient city's families' best
our p.c. children choose incest.

Melting in the Dark 3 [13]

The welded once offending severed hand
that held the water weapon wielded by the kid,
a symbol of the site of joy's last stand,
is now the subject of the highest auction bid.

O, if the mayor had only let the water freely run,
we would have had no fear of flagrant fountain gun.
The city's drought is patron to our art,
attaining affirmation at the e-bay mart.

Melting in the Dark 4 [14]

So auction off...or future war forsake.
From semi-automatic rifles make
a Guadalupe goddess virgin sculpture,
symbolic of our old Norteño culture.

And from the art's great judgment seat
where hand jobs sell, beware of the city street
where weapons, serpents, snakes and sex compete:
Our Bud's all balls and Sis is soon dead meat.

Melting in the Dark 5 [15]

Butt, what's this so stuffed in her back pocket?
the concealed twin of Bud's bedeviled rocket!
They say it is okay if she don't point it.
The venus penis reigns, so let's anoint it.

Living in the Lap of Luxury. [16]
It's for the Birds

1. The Early Bird Gets the Worm

At half past five in three o four quail run,
my mind awaits the meld of morning sun.
The early birds do not wake me at dawn.
Outside, there is no green inviting lawn
of worms to cultivate our feathered friends.
And so, my head works hard to make amends
for lack of noise of natural arousal
and substitutes instead this residual espousal:

It's not so strange to think of tiny song birds hiding
below a floor where no one seems to be residing.

2. In Winter I Get Up at Night

And so, at morning I arise at night
and stretch and flex by lamp and pale sky light,
then poke along the blackened asphalt trail
in slow pursuit the swallow's sailing tail
amid the chirps and trills and calls of birds at sky.
Beware the swoop of balls of golf that fly
and squishy poop of animals for which no owner
provides a scoop; alas, I am become a moaner;
for that which swiftly fills the gripping soles of running
    shoes
is not the sort of stuff that spurs the poet's muse.

3. There's No Place Like Home

Among the ducts and pipes and conduits
installed below the rafters underground,
the speeding sparrow flits and tweets and shits,
the product drops without much of a sound.
The purplish plops themselves provide the reason:
red berries in profusion in spring season.
While on the porch there's building in the awning;
the search for string and straw starts up at dawning.
In celebration of the balcony of nesting birds,
the rhyming couplet's proven best for pastoral words.

4. Road Kill

As suggested by stanzas one, two and three,
by early light of dawn, beyond the gate
that exiles each inmate
from reality,
appreciate the traffic of Old Pecos Trail:
the middle of the road kill is dead cottontail
with a hole in its head where an eye used to be,
by the beak of a black bird that pecks out soft tissue,
but birds are birds, so that is not the issue.
The sounds and songs of flight our hearts uplift,
while wildness calls to mind that life is just a gift.

5. **Sunday Morning**

To pursue on the Lord's Day two brown cowering
    bunnies
beats bright, green, wings of cockatoos and late Sunday
    funnies.
And on the balcony whereat I sat
Appears the pillows upon which they shat.
Apparently, our flitting friends prefer to perch
on backs of chairs in purchase of the perfect search
for seeds, or worms, or slugs or god-knows-what,
but, on the porch, to poop is oft the spot.
This verse upholds my woefully imperfect worder.
I think that I'll become an audobonic birder.

6. **What's in a Name?**

There seems to be no covey quail that seeks this place,
at least none come to sight in any walk or race
of mine. It's funny how they give a place a name.
If quail runs everywhere are just the same,
then who protects the copyrights of quails that run?
Perhaps no developer wants to be outdone.
Work out on weights and take a steaming shower.
Ignore bird identity; imbibe at happy hour.
Every builder wants to be a topnotcher.
Instead, I'll think I'll be a gimlet-eyed titwatcher.

7. Birds of a Feather, Flock Together

Steps past Zia East road dry river sand runs:
the choked arroyo de los chamisos suns,
a safari in the scorched serengeti,
or stage four on quail run's drought scarred grey green
 tee.
This is no place for birds to drink or fly.
The reason I am here at play begs "why?"
They spray the concrete arches scrawled with cultic
corners marked to signify graffiti ethnic…
Return! O topless towers of torreon
that they cannot afford, but we can own.

8. Somewhere Over the Rainbow

Between a blackbird, raven and a crow,
the difference, I think I'll never know,
despite the studies, photos and description.
The forager ignores the proscription:
"don't tread on me"; "keep off the grass";
and "feed not fish or fowl"; and "don't trespass."
It sits upon the green in majesty serene
and seeks with beak the worm as source protein.
That which it is does not show fear of man,
and that is how it is since time began.

There is no rainbow over which the bluebird flies;
the bird that's big and black controls the skies.

9. Bed in Summer

In May, I have to go to bed and see
the red-headed finch still hopping with esprit.
El sol does not sink early in the sky.
In summertime, I go to bed by day
and wake with the sun the same old way.
It takes no smarts for you to know just why:
I'm up from morning calls for scoring seeds,
undeterred birds, ignoring sacred sleeping needs,
to feed the wide and hungry mouths which cry.
Nothing like a little nesting sex succeeds.

10. The Mark of Cain

In fairway four dissolves a drying pond,
once filled with water product from the sky
that our forbears identified as rain
in days of yore when heavy clouds dropped down,
and wild birds fly from pond to far beyond.
Will life return to paradise again?
Or does our future lie in desert dust?
So is it still the God in whom we trust?
And like the dry that marks the ground of bloody Cain,
mankind, like birds, will live its life a vagabond.

11. Bye-Bye Baby Bunting, Daddy's Gone A'hunting

I ask: "when is a bunny not a beast?"
And nonsense says: "when coyote fails to feast."
For fences here are high, and wolves and deer
are simply not allowed to enter here,
unlike the flying not-a-beast, the birds,
or rabbits which, within their warrens, burrow
to veil from rubber wheels of tractors moved to mow.
And deer don't trail and drop dried turds
to be mistook for baby bunny eggs
that bear bubonic and assorted plagues.

12. Ten Little Indians

Electric lines are also buried underground.
Our tender ears don't hear the Taos humming sound.
And there is no offense by our eye sights' hellhound.
Around the boundary, the birds sit on a wire,
refugees from summer's fierce Borrego fire.
For seeds and rain the birds' brains' minds conspire.
Why does the scaled quail turn her head and run?
No place exists for beasts or birds in fire's sun.
For all the good that God can do, the sun's undone.
And like the "harvest" metaphor for killing whale,
too soon harpooned by men called Ahab and Ishmael,
as evidence of all earthbound men can do or fail,
the result is that, at end, there were exactly none.

THE GOOD,
THE BAD,
AND THE UGLY

"If Canyon Road has turned to prostituting herself (by tourist-trapping, the 'current dominant mode on Canyon Road'), space like this [the Van de Griff/Marr Gallery] are her proverbial heart of gold."
—*Critical Reflections*, Jon Carver, *THE magazine*.

"As the second most important art center in the United States, Santa Fe is…a place to view art of all kinds in a beautiful, easily walkable…historically important setting."
—*Santa Fe Gallery Association Guide*.

"It has been said, without much documentation, that Santa Fe is the country's No. 3 art center, after New York and Los Angeles," "Art Sells—Big Time."
—*New Mexico Business Journal*.

"The life of a city is its art. The art of a city is its life."
—*Tucson Guide*.

"Ogan [Larry Ogan, executive director of the Santa Fe Council for the Arts] said the current malaise for at least part of the local art industry follows a proliferation of art galleries in recent years, especially on Canyon Road. 'There's been a huge growth in galleries there, and a huge growth in rent,' he said, explaining that in some cases those higher rents are affordable only for well-established galleries with branches elsewhere." "The Worst of Times?"
—Bob Quick, *The Santa Fe New Mexican*.

"The 60 million subscribers to cable's Home & Garden Television channel will get a chance to take an armchair journey up Santa Fe's Canyon Road on the day after Thanksgiving. 'Dream Drives,' a program which explores 'fascinating neighborhoods that typically have one defining street, avenue or boulevard as their anchor,' taped a Canyon Road episode for the series, which has also visited such places as Los Angeles' Mulholland Drive, New Orleans' St. Charles Avenue and Washington, D.C.'s Embassy Row. A promo for the show describes Canyon Road as Santa Fe's 'premiere location for sophisticated homes and art galleries.'" "Road Trip."
—*El Mitote*, *The Santa Fe New Mexican*.

"A steady flow of affluent, art-obsessed pedestrians has turned once-rural Canyon Road into a handsome real estate investment for a widowed grocer's wife, a gutsy entrepreneur and a Fortune 500 company...LaRoche [painter Carol LaRoche] left after Gypsy Alley was purchased for renovation. A refinished, one-bedroom apartment on the alley, complete with hardwood floors and trendy, stainless steel appliances, now rents for $1,400 a month...David Ross (who sells functional animal art out of his home studio at 610 Canyon Road) said Conlon and Siegal's Gypsy Alley renovation paved over what had been a vital part of Canyon Road. 'It's taking a natural phenomenon and turning it into real estate,' Ross said. But Siegal says the buildings he renovated two years ago were 'adobe covered shacks' and 'tenement-quality' apartments. He's created four galleries and four apartments and said reactions to the new Gypsy Alley have been 'phenomenally positive.' 'It was a slum,' said Conlon. 'It's a beautiful little walking street now,'" "The Changing Face of Canyon Road."
—Morgan Lee, *Albuquerque Journal North*.

"It was a time when Canyon Road, the now world-famous street on Santa Fe's east side, was still called 'El Camino del Cañon,' its original name, and when houses along its path were still home to the families who built them.

"'It was all families then, uncles and aunts and cousins and grandparents,' says Valentina Ortiz," "Canyon Road's Roots Run Deep."
—Carmella M. Padilla, *Santa Fe Reporter*.

"Canyon Road may be the most sensually pleasing street in America," and "Upper Canyon retains much more of the European feel that once permeated all of Santa Fe."
—*Access Guide to Santa Fe, Taos, and Albuquerque*, Harper Collins Publishing.

"William Uriah Tate, 68, was among the last of the bohemian artists who set Santa Fe apart from the world. But 'bohemian artist' is too limiting a description. An adventurer and frontier man, Tate was sometimes ornery. His delightful irreverence kept in check the snooty art world that sprouted up around him...Tate who remembered Canyon Road when it was 'a barefoot lane, a never-never land...we gave Santa Fe a name as an art community all over the world,'" "Tate's Death Seals Off Link to City's Past."
—Cheryl Wittenauer, *The Santa Fe New Mexican*.

"When I arrived in 1964...I wandered into Claude's Bar...Claude James herself was sitting on a barstool. This was the remnants of her establishment [on Canyon Road]...that had, 15 years previously, been the exotic watering hole for an international set of lesbians. Claude, who had lived in Paris as a child, entertained her clientele with her renditions of Edith Piaf songs while cabrito roasted in a spit in the huge fireplace," "Remembering a Free Spirit."
—Jo Basiste, *Albuquerque Journal North*.

"The halo is history everywhere on Canyon Road."
—*Santa Fean*.

"Centuries ago, Canyon Road was used by Indians from Rio Grande pueblos as a principal route to the Pecos pueblos. Since then, it has seen armed conquistadores, warriors of Po-Pe, Mexican Regulars, men of the Confederacy and has served as a burro trail to the piñon-studded hills for those in search of firewood. Centuries-old adobe buildings such as El Zaguan at 545 Canyon, has created the architectural charm that is a hallmark of Canyon Road."
—*The Wingspread Guide to Canyon Road, The Art and Soul of Santa Fe.*

"The news on the block may have famous parents, but celebrity gawkers should put this aside and enjoy the sweetness and charm of owners Brooke Palance and Michael Wilding…Trixies has quickly become the 'number one place to be,'" Trixies Café, 822 Canyon Road.
—*THE Magazine*.

"'Contemporary art is very, very hard to sell,' [Bunny] Conlon said. 'I have no desire to take on art that is sellable just because it's sellable. I get a lot of compliments but not enough sales,'" "Conlon Half of Conlon-Siegel Galleries Closing."
—Hollis Walker, *The Santa Fe New Mexican*.

"The real movers and shakers in Santa Fe aren't on Canyon Road," BTHomes advertisement.
—*The Santa Fe New Mexican*.

"The Historic Neighborhood Association is on alert. Not for crime, but for 'made in Taiwan' stickers. The group has lobbied the city to help ensure that business on Canyon Road lives up to its reputation," "Canyon Road Watchdog."
—Marie Luisa Tucker, *Santa Fe Reporter*.

NOTES ON THE POEMS

1.
Naked Ladies on the Road

"Some folks claim there are legends in Native American tribes that speak of a 'Pale Prophet' that once visited our homelands and taught his virtuous and righteous ways throughout the North and South American continents. These legends tell of a healer, a saintly white man who performed miracles," "Jesus and the Three Indian Guys," Harlan McKosato, *The Santa Fe New Mexican.*

"It's a load of dung. More specifically: It is elephant feces glued to the Virgin Mary's breast, a collage by British painter Chris Ofili, and it has launched the bloodiest culture war skirmish since Andres Serrano's 'Piss Christ,'" *U.S. News and World Report.*

"Our town's commotion hasn't reached the proportions of the one at the Brooklyn Museum of Art in New York, but it brings up the same issues of freedom of expression, tolerance and moral standards," "College Must Stand for Freedom, Tolerance," Editorial, *The Santa Fe New Mexican.*

"There's a great deal of racism and classism going on in northern New Mexico that remains unacknowledged," said Aline Brandauer, curator of contemporary art at the Museum of Fine Arts. "The museum system perpetuates that by the way it divides up objects that belong to it," "Performance Artist Targets Stereotypes," *Albuquerque Journal North.*

"A deacon and members of Our Lady of Guadalupe parish in Santa Fe are voicing disapproval of a computer-collage in a state museum depicting the Virgin of Guadalupe in a floral bikini, held aloft by a bare breasted saint.... The image (1531 version) now graces everything from church sanctuaries and holy cards to T-shirts, low riders and mouse pads," "Skimpily Attired 'Our Lady' Protested," Morgan Lee, *Albuquerque Journal North*.

"Thou shalt have no other gods before me. Thou shalt not make unto thee a graven image, nor any manner of likeness, of anything that is in heaven above, or that is in the earth beneath, or that is in the water under the earth; thou shalt not bow down unto them, nor serve them," Exodus 20:3.

"'*Nuevo Mexicanos* have always had to fight that,' [Tey Marianna] Nunn [curator of contemporary Hispano and Latino collections at the Museum of International Folk Art] acknowledged. 'We have a long history of oppression, of people from the outside coming in and taking over. I completely understand that I spend most of my time fighting that myself,'" "Virgin Controversy Comes to Boil at Rally," *The Santa Fe New Mexican*.

"I wore a miniskirt and combat boots.... All people see is a female physique—the devil's playground. It's that fine line in our culture where we have been endlessly judged as either a virgin or a harlot. There's never been an in-between. Yet God created the human body, so why is it considered evil?" "'Our Lady' Feud, the Latest Battle in Ancient War on Sexuality," Goldie Garcia, *The Albuquerque Tribune*.

"My *Virgen de Guadalupe* is not the mother of God. She is God," *Guadalupe the Sex Goddess*, Sandra Cisneros.

"The Aztecs, Incas and Mayans all worshipped the moon as a fertility goddess. The Catholic Church needed to co-opt that indigenous image to help along what was a hostile, military takeover of the native people and the lands," "Liturgical Art a Potent Force in History," *The Santa Fe New Mexican*.

"Museum of New Mexico Regent Frank V. Ortiz…compared a state museum exhibit to racial epithets and suggested Hispanic representation among docents is inadequate…. 'At issue is whether or not a state funded museum in interpreting curatorial rights granted by the First Amendment uses sound judgment when it exhibits works equivalent to the impact of 'Savages,' 'Niggers,' 'faggots,' 'Kikes,' 'Dikes' [sic], 'Greasers,' in the community at large,' Ortiz wrote," "Regent Under Fire for Attack on Exhibit, Volunteers," *Albuquerque Journal North*.

"Archbishop Michael Sheehan…likened the artwork to portraying the mother of Jesus 'as a prostitute,'" "'Our Lady' Will Stay at Museum," *Albuquerque Journal North*.

"I'm tempted to throw in my lipstick case and compete for mayoral votes, too. I'd campaign wearing a floral bikini and give my speeches standing on an orange barrel," "Candidates Abound, But What I Want Is a Knight," Goldie Garcia, *The Albuquerque Tribune*.

"Christians instantly recognize this as one of the Beatitudes, the Commandments of Blessedness. But perhaps some have forgotten it in the still-bubbling conflict over the digital image 'Our Lady' at the Museum of International Folk Art in Santa Fe," "Museum's 'Our Lady' Decision Was Righteous," Editorial, *The Albuquerque Tribune*.

"'Our culture is under attack,' said Richard Medina, one of the marchers.... Anthony Trujillo, a deacon at our Lady of Guadalupe in Santa Fe, helped spearhead Saturday's march. He said the exhibit is offensive to local Hispanics for a lot of reasons," "Marchers Vow to Persevere," *The Sunday Journal North*.

"In the name of the *Virgencita de Guadalupe*...I confess that I am a *Guadalupana* and a Buddhist. Bless me Guadalupe-Tonantzin, for I do not pray to you the way my mother does. I see you as the female face of sacred life, Grandmother Earth; the feminine presence of God, of Life, or Creation itself.... My ancient soul yearns for the sacred feminine energies inside the earth, the moon, the universe, and I pray 'the Indian way' of my ancestors for all these things. By honoring the feminine energies, I honor myself as woman." "Guadalupe Represents Feminine Energy of God," Patricia Gonzales, *Albuquerque Journal*.

"All the mendicant orders...considered the [Virgin Mary of Guadalupe] cult to be idolatrous.... The Los Angeles County Museum of Art now displays a cutting-edge image, *Nuestra Madre*, in which Guadalupe is a bare-breasted clone of a Star Wars creature with Mexican features. The Alma López image...is benign by contrast," Jacqueline Orsini Dunnington, Letter to the Editor, *THE magazine*.

2.
You've Just Got to Love Their Lingo

"'Well, the big hangout was Claude's,' he said. 'Claude was one crazy lady. Her big thing was she liked to cook and raise Yorkshire terriers. Once she even opened a pet shop next to the bar. What a misadventure that was.'" *Pasatiempo, The Santa Fe New Mexican*

3.
The Saga of Gypsy Alley

"Milton! Thou shouldst be living at this hour: England hath need of thee," "To Milton," William Wordsworth.

"We never had plans to be a landlord.... I feel bad but it would have happened anyway. If we don't buy it someone from the outside might plow the buildings down or build condos," "The Last Affordable Canyon Art Space," Dottie Indyke, *Pasatiempo, The Santa Fe New Mexican*.

"He [Stuart Ashman] identified the flavor as characterized by her interest in artists working on the edge of contemporary art—artists whose work includes significant social or emotional content.... She wasn't as concerned with 'design,'" he added. Conlon also wasn't as concerned with sales," "Bunny Conlon: Visionary Presence in Art Scene/ Closes Her Doors on Feb. 1," Craig Smith, *Pasatiempo, The Santa Fe New Mexican*.

"The modern movement in art has for years sought to deal with its aesthetic and intellectual exhaustion through provocative and politically motivated works that substitute ideas for 'art'—but ideas of a banality, even puerility, that demonstrate the movement's terminal crisis.

"If these artists' political views were of some political weight, one could respect them, whatever the aesthetic nullity of the works produced. Unfortunately, they usually are intellectually trivial: intentionally scandalous attacks on sexism, capitalism, racism, religion, war, imperialism, homophobia, censorship and other fashionable objects of elite outrage.

"The art movements that have followed (to abbreviate the story) failed to establish a firm claim to aesthetic succession. This is why the politicized art of the present day evades the aesthetic question by changing categories. It demands to be judged as political action, rather than as art.

"When it is so judged, the verdict must be that there is little or nothing there. It provides the demonstration of modernism's crisis," "Polemics, Shock Value Cover Up Artists' Aesthetics Poverty," William Pfaff, *The Sunday Journal.*

"Many people don't express their creative spirit because they have been intimidated by the art world into believing art is the exclusive realm of pretentious artists, wealthy connoisseurs and snooty critics who fill their reviews with foreign phrases and pointless anecdotes about Paris.

"Some artists compound the problem by issuing manifestos that 'explain' their art with five-syllable words and unintelligible phrases, the more obscure the better. The unwashed masses just aren't welcome anymore, unless you can spare $50,000 for the latest *piece de résistance*," "What a Crock. Art Belongs to Anyone, Everyone," Brendan Smith, *The Hitching Post, Albuquerque Journal North.*

4.
Plumbing Crisis

"[A] problem is [that] a sewer service line required all water to be shut off at City Hall and a new 60-foot trench to be dug…area archaeologists believe that a relatively old and fairly large pueblo is located under the City Hall in Santa Fe's downtown," "Plumbing Crisis Yields Opportunity," *Albuquerque Journal North*.

5.
How Santa Klaus Came to the Kremlin

"Karen Walker is moving to…Delgado St. 'It's right next to the bridge where the bomb secrets were given away,' Walker said," "Real Estate Moves to New Space," *The Santa Fe New Mexican*.

"Barring some miraculous evidence—say, a photo of Wen Ho Lee having drinks with Julius and Ethel Rosenberg at the Delgado Bridge—the government's handling of the…case continues to amaze me," "Only in Santa Fe," Denise Kusel, *The Santa Fe New Mexican*.

"Forever after, Greenglass would be known as the guy who saved his own life by sending his sister to the electric chair.… 'All I want,' Greenglass said…'is to be forgotten.… My wife is more important to me than my sister,'" Book review of *The Brother: The Untold Story of Atomic Spy David Greenglass*, James R. Peipert, Knight Ridder Newspapers, *Albuquerque Journal North*.

"Rhodes [Richard Rhodes, winner of the Pulitzer in 1986 for *The Making of the Atomic Bomb*] also criticized the executions of Julius and Ethel Rosenberg, who helped leak the secrets. Rhodes said he thinks their execution was unfair because Fuchs, who was directly responsible for the theft of the Los Alamos secrets, escaped with a relatively light prison sentence. 'Their execution was a Cold War tragedy and travesty,' he said," "Author: Fear Drove Atomic Spying," Kahthleene Parker, *The Santa Fe New Mexican*.

"At the heart of the Los Alamos leaks was British scientist Klaus Fuchs and another as yet unknown spy called Perseus.... 'He was an American born physicist who is still living. He might be in the audience today,' Rhodes said." *Ibid.*

For identification of the Castillo Bridge and the whereabouts of its remains, see "The Atomic Spies," Tom Sharpe, and "Spies Were Willing But Not So Able," *Albuquerque Journal North*. For the Harry Gold-David Greenglass Albuquerque connection, see Sharpe, above, and "The Spies Upstairs," Ollie Reed, Jr., *The Albuquerque Tribune*.

6.
Epitaph for Escondido

"A group of citizens on Camino Escondido withdrew their application for a rezoning Wednesday after the Santa Fe City Council moved toward splitting up the zoning on the one-block street off Canyon Road. Leonard Katz, representing the group, said 21 of the 27 property owners wanted to remove the commercial arts-and-crafts overlay on the street while it remained all residential. He said the group feared an influx of galleries like those on Canyon Road." "Rezoning Withdrawn," *The Santa Fe New Mexican.*

Mayor Larry Delgado voted in favor of those who opposed keeping Camino Escondido residential. Delgado broke a tie City Council vote in favor of commercialism, saying 'he was tired of hearing people bash Canyon Road and use it as a bad example.

7.
La Acequia Madre
(The Mother Ditch)

"[A]cequia is an Arabic word meaning shared water resource. The acequia system to irrigate farm land, which makes agriculture possible in a desert environment such as New Mexico, was introduced by the Spanish in 1598, when the first irrigation ditch was dug in Chamita, near Santa Cruz. The acequias are the core institution of the Indo-Hispano culture," "Acequias Celebrated In Taos," *Albuquerque Journal North*.

"La Villa Real de la Santa Fe de San Francisco de Asis, Nuevo Mejico, was founded on Roman Catholic Spanish values, norms, customs and traditions.... Santa Fe's Hispano people will always continue to preserve our rich spiritual beliefs and tradition," Joseph Vigil, Letter to the Editor, *The Santa Fe New Mexican*.

"By the rivers of Babylon, there we sat down, yea, we wept, when we remembered Zion," Psalms 137:1.

**8.
Rites of Passage**

"'What we must do is to work together with landowners and all concerned to bring down all those needless fences erected by hate, by greed, by superstition, by prejudice, all those fences that, without cause or justification, hurt and exclude,' Bob French told a group of neighbors who met Saturday…on Camino Militar, just off upper Canyon Road," "Some Fences Don't Make for Good Neighbors," *The Santa Fe New Mexican.*

Poem of The Cid, English Verse Translation and with an introduction by W.S. Merwin, New American Library, 1959.

9.
El Camino del Cañon

"It is the now-paved end of an old Indian trail that ran along the Santa Fe River from Pecos Pueblo in Santa Fe. *El Camino del Cañon*, its original name, was a Spanish-of-the-Spanish street until early in this century, when Eastern-bred artists discovered it," Kate McGraw, *Santa Fe Reporter.*

10.
Remarks at Pecos National Monument

"I wanted to remind my fellow Journal readers of an oversight in the recent news stories about the remains of Indians from Pecos Pueblo being 'returned'—to Jemez Pueblo! Most of the descendants of Pecos Pueblo do not live at Jemez Pueblo, but in the region surrounding Pecos Pueblo. Years before the final inhabitants of that pueblo moved to Jemez Pueblo, many of the Pecos Indians married into neighboring mixed Indian-Spanish families and chose to be considered Spanish, with the Catholic Church's blessing, and lived as Spanish and then Mexican, and finally American citizens. Today the Pueblo's descendants are still there, near the old pueblo, living normal American lives," Bert Olinger, "Pecos Descendants Still Live in Area," Letter to the Editor, *Albuquerque Journal North*.

11.
Melting in the Dark 1

"The deadlocked water battle that has raged for two decades in Santa Fe's historical Guadalupe Neighborhood will soon bow to current sensitivities...the statue called 'The Children's Fountain of Santa Fe' in West De Vargas Park will be disarmed...artist Linda Strong has decided to hack off the water pistol that the bronze version of her son uses in an eternal water fight with his sister," "Statue of Boy to Be Disarmed," *Albuquerque Journal North*.

"'I want this piece of bronze, because, I believe, that the right of the people to keep and bear arms shall not be infringed—amputated,' [Libertarian Party legislative candidate John] McEnroe said," "Candidate Wants Squirt Gun," *Albuquerque Journal North*.

"MacArthur's Park is melting in the dark," "MacArthur Park" written by Jimmy Webb, best known as recorded by Donna Summer.

"But if any harm follow, then thou shalt give life for life, eye for eye, tooth for tooth, hand for hand, foot for foot, burning for burning, wound for wound, stripe for stripe." Exodus 21:24.

"And if thy right hand offend thee, cut it off, and cast it from thee," Matthew 5:29; to same effect, Mark 9:47.

12.
Melting in the Dark 2

"A phallic symbol?! George W. Rogers (letter, Aug. 18) sees the garden hose that Linda Strong replaced the water pistol with as a phallic symbol? Gee, I uh, well I always thought a garden hose looked like just that, a garden hose. But maybe that is because my apparently naive mind is in the garden and not the gutter." Letter to the Editor, *The Santa Fe New Mexican*.

"[B]ut of the fruit of the tree which is in the midst of the garden, God hath said: Ye shall not eat of it, neither shall ye touch it, lest ye die." Genesis 3:3. "And the Lord God said unto the woman: What hast thou done? And the woman said: The serpent beguiled me, and I did eat." Genesis 3:13.

13.
Melting in the Dark 3

"The bronze hand wielding a water pistol that was amputated from a Santa Fe fountain last year is still intended to go to a higher bidder.... Critics contended the water pistol appeared to be a real gun when the fountain wasn't running with water," "Sculpture's Hand May Go on Sale," *Albuquerque Journal North*.

"I've struggled all my life with why I wasn't getting recognition.... I got to the point where I was feeling like giving up. I was looking for affirmation from others, and I wasn't getting it," "New York Artist Finds a Home in New Mexico, Only in Santa Fe," Denise Kusel, *The Santa Fe New Mexican*.

14.
Melting in the Dark 4

"Last week wasn't the first time the Española City Council has voted to auction confiscated guns.... A residents group also has been working on a plan to use the guns to make a sculpture of the Virgin of Guadalupe as a message against violence.... The four councilors who voted for the auction argued that it won't include small-caliber handguns often used in the commission of crimes. But the auction lot does include 63 larger-caliber handguns, including semi-automatics, all of which have already been used in crimes," "Rethink Vote On Gun Auction," Editorial, *Albuquerque Journal North*.

"Oh, East is East and West is West, and never the twain shall meet, / Til Earth and Sky stand presently at God's great Judgment Seat," *The Ballad of East and West*, Rudyard Kipling, 1889.

15.
Melting in the Dark 5

"In April, Gov. Gary Johnson signed into law the Concealed Handgun Carry Act, which permits approved state residents to carry concealed, loaded handguns," "Mayor Proposes Concealed Handgun Ban," *Albuquerque Journal*.

16.
Living in the Lap of Luxury.
It's for the Birds

Torreon—fortified towers built by early Hispanic communities as lookouts and refuges against constant Indian danger.

"When thou tillest the ground, it shall not henceforth yield unto thee her strength; a fugitive and a vagabond shalt thou be in the earth," Genesis 4:12.

"Today the annual rate of extinction is 1,000 to 10,000 times faster than during the past half-billion years, writes E.O. Wilson in his latest book, *The Future of Life*. If nothing more is done, one-fifth of all the plants and animal species now on earth could be gone or on the road to extinction by 2030," Editor's Note, *Audubon*.

www.ingramcontent.com/pod-product-compliance
Lightning Source LLC
Chambersburg PA
CBHW021018090426
42738CB00007B/815